CENTRAL BRISTOL THROUGH THE AGES

Anthony Beeson

AMBERLEY

To the Shade of John Herbert Beeson (1909 – 1963), my father, whose
journey ended too soon.

Oh, loving Soul, my own so tenderly,
My life's companion and my body's guest,
To what new realms, poor flutterer, wilt thou fly?
Cheerless, disrobed, and cold in thy lone quest,
Hushed thy sweet fancies, mute thy wonted jest.

P. Aelius Hadrianus Imp.
—D. Johnston (translation)

First published 2017

Amberley Publishing
The Hill, Stroud
Gloucestershire, GL5 4EP

www.amberley-books.com

ISBN 978 1 4456 5365 5 (print)
ISBN 978 1 4456 5366 2 (ebook)

British Library Cataloguing in Publication Data.
A catalogue record for this book is available from
the British Library.

Origination by Amberley Publishing.
Printed in the UK.

Introduction

It is inevitable that cities change with time. As this volume is written another series of redevelopments are underway in Bristol at sites in Rupert and Redcliff Streets that will further change it.

I first visited Bristol in 1966 as an eighteen-year-old on holiday from Brighton and staying with relatives in Somerset. I particularly wanted to visit Blaise Castle to see what Jane Austen's delightful heroine in *Northanger Abbey* had been wild to experience and yet never achieved. I little realised then that within seven years I would be living adjacent to Blaise Woods. Arriving at Temple Meads railway station I remember being surprised to hear that Bristol's new bus station, required for the next stage of my journey, had not been built adjoining Temple Meads (which might have been sensible), but involved a bus ride to reach it. Bristolians seemed helpful and friendly and once en route to the bus station I passed the sad boarded-up buildings of the Lewin's Mead area. A fellow passenger informed me that they were soon to be replaced by a grand new scheme. On a subsequent visit that week, to seek out the elusive (and still neglected) ruins of Bristol Castle, I recall being impressed by the view from Union Street of the elevated glass walkway spanning Fairfax Street from Fairfax House. Fritz Lang's *Metropolis* and those imagined cities of the future with skyscrapers linked by elevated ways that appeared in 1950s children's encyclopaedias sprang to my teenage mind. Brighton certainly had nothing comparable!

Until the 1820s much of Bristol's medieval, Tudor and Jacobean architecture remained, making the city a curiosity to visitors. Most found the buildings interesting but some, like the visiting Londoner James Malcolm in 1805, found them 'grotesque and encroaching' and could not wait for a time when they were as rare in Bristol as the Great Fire had made them in London. They would approve of today's Bristol. The terrible bombing of the Second World War is often blamed for the lack of early architecture in Bristol's central area, but in reality Bristolians themselves were demolishing ancient buildings up until the Blitz and far beyond. The nineteenth century and early twentieth century saw whole areas change from domesticity to industry with new factories replacing the old streets and courts, and we are indebted to those who thought to record the city's antiquities in art and photography. Unlike in similar bombed towns in Germany, there was no plan here to restore and replicate historic buildings such as the Dutch House. A Bristol for a new age was planned, but with neither the funds nor the genius to successfully achieve it. Indeed when I took up the position of Fine Art Librarian at the Central Library in 1972, a senior colleague informed me that in its pursuit of the new Bristol it was, allegedly, the planning department's mantra to demolish anything old that the Germans had missed. Looking at the devastation inflicted on some areas of the city for the sake of the new road system and 'temporary' car parks, it was easy to imagine that this might indeed be the unofficial truth.

Bristol has evolved greatly since the 1970s. The conversion of the docks from commerce to pleasure and domesticity has had much to do with this. Redevelopment and gentrification has seen a population again inhabiting inner-city areas that had previously lost almost all their inhabitants. More mixed redevelopment rather than the inevitable office blocks that turn areas of a city into ghost towns out of business hours have slowly emerged. Visually Bristol appears cleaner, brighter and more beautiful. Older Britons can remember when most town buildings were black with air pollution (see the old Council House on page 13). The city is certainly less aromatic than a century ago. As late as the 1960s the General Hospital was forced to shut its windows during heatwaves because of the stench arising from the adjacent harbour. Those connected with improving the city's environment are to be praised. The official changing of the historic name of Bristol's Council House to the Americanised 'City Hall' has had little effect on Bristolians beyond wondering how much the reprinting of the council's stationery cost the 'Green City'.

Culturally, and futuristically, the blow suffered by the people's Central Library must raise the utmost concern. The surrendering of its lower floors and the relocation of a great proportion of its rare reference and periodical stock to the B Bond Warehouse at Hotwells, to which only a minority of the staff have access, has severe implications for the service. Notwithstanding the obvious inconvenience to Bristolians (who own the book-stock), the vital element of libraries is their staff's knowledge of the books and their contents, under their care, and only gained by daily familiarity. Staff shortages have made training visits to the relocated book-stock impossible. While older library staff may retain knowledge of items, for their successors it will be a case of 'out of sight out of mind' and the value of the collections will wither. For the Bristol historian many local newspapers have been microfilmed. However, tightly bound originals or damaged or substandard film means that sections are often illegible. Reference staff would previously then consult the bound archival copy. Now, however, these archival newspapers are banished to A Bond Warehouse. The specially designed enamelled-steel 'bins' that once shelved them were scrapped and the great volumes are now piled on concrete floors in non-archival conditions with a directive that not even staff are to consult them and that enquirers should be sent on to the British Library.

This volume is arranged as a series of textual peregrinations around the city. The illustrations are mostly from the author's collection and that of the Central Reference Library. In addition I would like to thank Antony Berridge, Jane Bradley, Julia Carver, Jacqueline Claridge, Dawn Dyer, Mia Hale, David Nelmes, Rosemary Scott, Karin Walton and John Williams.

Baldwin Street to Broad Plain

In Baldwin Street, 1896

Baldwin Street's western extension to the Centre opened in 1881. From this date the remaining vacant building lots (such as appears on the left, cornering Marsh Street) gradually filled with a selection of commercial buildings and offices. St Stephen's Chambers (otherwise 'Dunlop Buildings' and later, St Stephen's Restaurant), John Bevan's 1879–81 Loiresque creation on the opposite corner, was owned by the wine merchants Dunlop and Mackie. Its attic storey was a riot of chimneys and cupola-topped turrets. The façade of The People's Palace music hall dominates the far right. Designed by James Hutton in 1892 for the Livermore Brothers' theatrical empire, its name originally featured in polychrome brick across the now painted and altered façade. For many years the Gaumont cinema, it has served other uses and in 2016 is unoccupied but extant. Only one property now remains from the terrace of three elegant Grecian houses seen distantly in St Augustine's Parade.

Hurrah for the Jubilee! 1897

The patriotically garlanded offices of the *Western Daily Press* at Nos 27–31 Baldwin Street, as recorded on a souvenir card commemorating Queen Victoria's Diamond Jubilee. The newspaper was first published in June 1858 at a time when Bristol boasted eight other journals. In 1859 the proprietors started the *Bristol Observer* and in 1877 the *Bristol Evening News*. Their offices were in Broad Street until 1885 when a building site was purchased from the Corporation for £8,000 at the confluence of the redeveloped Baldwin Street with St Stephen Street. The building survived the Blitz but, in 1959, the newspaper was bought by Bristol United Press and subsequently published, with the *Evening Post,* from offices in Temple Way. In 1999 Bristol United Press was acquired by the Daily Mail and General Trust. Subsequent economies saw printing and even the editorial office removed from Bristol. The latter has now returned. Sadly in 1965 Newminster House replaced the old building.

'A look of vulnerable preciosity'
Hemmed in by mediocre post-war
neighbours, the premises of fruit merchants
T. Mansfield and Son at No. 40 Baldwin
Street awaits its inevitable fate in Jim Hale's
1960s photograph. Mansfield's striking
façade of cut Bath stone and rough pennant
originally fronted a leather warehouse when
it was built in the late 1870s. To the right
appears the bland façade of the Equity and
Law Building, while to the left the more
substantial Royal London Building that
replaced Canada House. Baldwin Street's
route from Welsh Back originally curved into
what is now St Stephen's Street. From 1874
it was redeveloped, widened and redirected,
slicing through many historic buildings on
its straightened route to Broad Quay. Like
Victoria Street, its brick and stone office
buildings and warehouses formed a visual
unit that was first damaged by the Blitz
and later by redevelopment. Mansfield's,
when demolished, became a car park, and a
postmodern arch now straddles its entrance.

7

The Prospect to Bridge Street Backs

'The view from the bridge of that noble pile of buildings on the lower side of Bridge-street ... must be pleasing to spectators', declared Mathews Bristol Guide in 1819. The rear façades of the Paty brothers' elegant 1760s street crowned the cliff overlooking the service road that backed them. Bridge Street replaced the earlier thoroughfare known as the Shambles or Worshipful Street. To the left above the transit shed appears a scaffolding-encased chimney from Fry's Pithay chocolate factory. Through the vessel's rigging peeps St Mary-Le-Port's tower while St Peter's appears left of the Bank Hotel that itself angles riverwards at the end of the terrace on the right. St Peter's Hospital closes that side of the river. On the extreme right of the photograph are the warehouses of Penner Wharf. Here, adjoining the original bridge, had once stood the spectacular 'Great House at the Bridge End'. Most of what appears here perished in the Second World War or was demolished thereafter.

St Nicholas on the Wall; Danger Replaced by Elegance

'The interior effect is that of an ornate assembly room, and, considered ... worthy of some toleration' was J. F. Nicholls' and John Taylor's verdict in 1881. Certainly the interior of the rebuilt church of 1764, with its elegant ceiling and froth of plasterwork by Thomas Stocking, bore little relationship to James Bridges' sober exterior and Thomas Paty's tower and spire. Only the crypt remained of the original church built on the city wall. Before 1762, those approaching Bristol's remarkable bridge would be confronted by St Nicholas Gate (below), which lay beneath the raised chancel of the church. Confined and dangerous, it caused many fatalities among riders and pedestrians. John Wesley narrowly escaped death here when pulled from his horse by a waggon. With the replacement of the bridge, the gate was also demolished to widen High Street and the church was rebuilt. Gutted in the Blitz it later became a splendid ecclesiastical museum until considered 'uneconomic'.

The Church of S.t NICHOLAS.

A Lottery at the Queen Bess Tavern, *c.* 1828

John Willis Snr, (fourth from left) painted this early private art union draw now in the city's collection. Customs officer Robert Emmett studies the prize. Members paid a small annual subscription and a contemporary artwork was purchased and awarded via a lottery. The named participants include picture dealer George Burge (sitting far right next to his brother William), three customs men and the landlord, Henry Gibbs (second left), and his wife. The ancient inn, once the home of John Whitson, founder of the Red Maids School, stood between Corn and Nicholas streets and was entered from both. Its central galleried courtyard boasted trees, open staircases, Tudor windows and gables and was compared to Southwark's Tabard. The landlord prospered, providing dinners for tradesmen and market people. A newspaper correspondent in 1880 recalled seeing a game called 'bull' (possibly 'Ringing the Bull') played there. Altered, then demolished for the Athenaeum (from 1889, the Liberal Club), the site still serves the public.

'Too much in turtle Bristol's Sons delight'

Until its demolition in 1854 Corn Street's Bush Tavern (recorded here by J. H. Maggs) was one of Britain's most famous and busiest coaching inns, even making an appearance in *The Pickwick Papers*. Its booking office placed travellers on coaches departing from outside to a dozen destinations countrywide. Services to Bath ran half-hourly. John Weeks, its irrepressible late-Georgian landlord and brother of Philip Weeks of Shirehampton's Lamplighters, offered guests a staggering menu. At Christmas anything from bustard to land tortoise, peahens and cuckoos were on offer. Turtles were a Bristol speciality and Wednesdays and Saturdays the Bush supplied them live or potted up to be sent to any destination. The railway ultimately ruined business and the building was replaced by Gingell and Lysaght's amazing paean to Sansovino's Venetian library, with its allegorical sculpture in honour of West Country Commerce and Industry by John Evan Thomas. The original five-bay bank façade was later extended by an entrance in Portland stone.

'...exceedingly beautiful ... more than anything ... seen elsewhere'

'Wonderful! that the citizens of Bristol should expend £50,000 on an Exchange erected by Wood of Bath, and yet prefer the rough stones of the street to the smooth ones of their piazzas and the casual torrents of a British climate'. James Malcolm, in 1805, was one of many visitors who admired the Corn Exchange but mocked Bristol's merchants who, afraid of missing out on a deal, after sixty years still congregated in the streets outside where trading had traditionally been conducted. This same fear of losing business kept many merchants living within the old city to the ruination of the developers building new estates in St Pauls, Kingsdown and Clifton. Edward Bird's recording shows the magnificent forum-like piazza as it appeared around 1815. It was roofed (and aesthetically ruined) in 1872, notwithstanding fears that this comfort might encourage farmers to gossip and loiter. Today it houses the Covered Market of independent retailers.

Disorder in Bristol: 'The evil influences of the Communists'

Bristol shared in the miseries of the Depression. Use of the Central Library's services rocketed with 9,500 visitors to the Newsroom to check job vacancies recorded in one day. The year 1932 saw several processions and subsequent disorder. On 9 February a strike by newsboys saw a demonstration in Horsefair organised by the National Workers' Unemployed Association. 'Communist speeches' were reportedly given and 4,000 demonstrators processed to the Council House (below in 1913), where councillors were debating reducing unemployment benefit. A deputation was refused admittance and the procession redirected to Old Market by police. When demonstrators attempted to reach the city centre, police drew truncheons and charged, reinforced by mounted officers. American newspapers reported thirty demonstrators and some police injured. Another demonstration on 25 February saw £300 of damage to shop windows. On 24 August a deputation stormed the Council Chamber following the decision to cut relief. A police baton charge allowed councillors to escape the attendant crowds.

13

In St Mary-le-Port Street, 1925
James Hill's photograph of the tall and picturesque
Jacobean buildings that were built against and
masked the north side of St Mary-le-Port Church.
Left of centre, a lantern hangs above the arched,
pedimented and gated entrance to the virtually
hidden church. Below the hanging sign for a
wholesale sweet merchant was the western entrance
to a lane that skirted the rectangular churchyard
and joined a flight of steps on the southern side
descending to Bridge Street. To the right, Georgian
brick buildings lead the eye to the pedimented
façade of the eastern entrance of the Flower Market.
Signs hang outside of Stevens Brothers' grocery
shops. Two of these Georgian buildings survived
the firestorm of 24 November 1940, but were later
demolished. The carriageway itself was removed in
1963. The current presentation of what was one of
Bristol's earliest streets illustrates the total lack of
historic empathy felt by post-war planners.

Sold: a Unique Corner Site, 1936

It is an unfortunate fact that many of Bristol's most historic buildings fell not through enemy action but at the hands of its native developers. Four years before the devastation of the Blitz, this photograph shows the ancient Swan Hotel and neighbouring properties in St Mary-le-Port Street at the junction with Bridge, Dolphin and Peter streets prior to demolition and the building of a new Saxone Shoes shop. A striped band running around the building and its neighbours designated which were to go. Sale notices boasted that 134 feet of shop frontage was included in the 5,260-square-foot site. Hodder's butchers' corner-shop, and the medieval Swan hotel vaults were included. The Swan was said to date from before 1434. It had a Georgian façade on Bridge Street that appears on the business card below, but the entrance through the Tudor façade appears at the right above. St Peter's tower appears beyond.

BANK HOTEL, BRIDGE STREET,
FIVE MINUTES DRIVE   E. DATE, *Proprietor*.   FROM THE RAILWAY STATION.

Two Funerals and a Fire-Escape

On 1 October 1870, Richard Williams, of The Bank Commercial Hotel, Bridge Street, died aged forty-nine. Remarkably his brother and joint proprietor, John, died less than three hours later in the hotel, aged forty-six. Adjoining St Peter's Hospital, the hotel overlooked the river, 'being in the heart of the city and in close proximity to the banks and principal warehouses and places of business'. It contained commercial, coffee and smoking rooms, stock and sitting rooms, and twenty-eight bedrooms. The 'second to none' billiard room (left above) boasted 'tables by Bennett'. By 1875 the proprietor was Mrs Date, whose business card, by Ensor, appears here. In the distance appears Counterslip's sugar refinery. In 1898 'the finest luncheon bar in the provinces' and a new restaurant were added. On 18 February 1893, City Road's Mr Jewell exhibited his 'Jewel Fire-Escape' here, descending from a top window while clasping a child. The hotel was bombed on 14 November 1940.

'Everything you might need from the cradle to the grave – all under one roof'
The Co-op's gift to the new Bristol in March 1962 was Fairfax House, built on the sinuous site between Narrow Wine and Fairfax streets and seen here from Dolphin Street. The River Frome flows through the site, which caused problems in construction, while the city wall and Newgate Prison had also stood here. The Co-op's façade sported great windows and easily cleanable glass mosaic. The six-storey store boasted a multistorey car park and a 'space-age' glazed bridge spanning Fairfax Street. Although it included a Saturday night dance floor, the instore miniature railway, Japanese tea garden and an attached cinema and restaurant complex were unrealised additions to what was hoped could become 'Bristol's Piccadilly Circus'. Internally it proved difficult to negotiate the various levels, or to even locate exits. Constantly moving 'up-and-over' Paternoster lifts terrified some shoppers. In 1985, Ladbroke City and County Land purchased Fairfax House and it was demolished for The Galleries development in 1988.

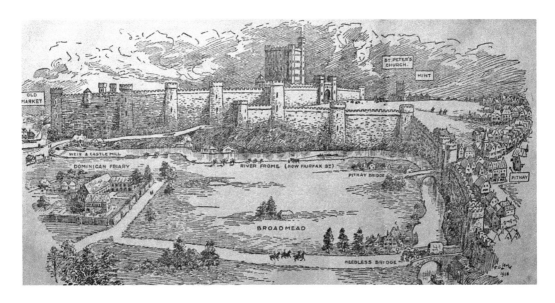

Bristol in the Middle Ages: the Prospect from Kingsdown

Frederick George Lewin's reconstruction of Bristol's royal castle and adjacent city. Although speculative in detail, it wonderfully illustrates how both castle and city crowned the hill and dominated the surrounding countryside to the north. Buildings now mask the considerable drop that exists between the castle plateau and the meadows of Broadmead. To the right of the castle, the earliest part of Bristol, dominated by St Peter's Church, appears. The Pithay curves downwards on the far right to its bridge over the Frome. Below the castle walls on the left a road (Broad Weir) climbs the hill towards Newgate, passing the weir and castle mill. The Frome, now below Fairfax Street, washes the outer circuit of the city walls in its course. The Dominican Friary (Quaker's Friars) sits near-left among the meadows. A bastion and outlines of the castle walls appear on the 1960s card, looking up Broad Weir to the site of Newgate by Fairfax House.

At Vosper Paget's Café, 1905

'We often go in to here to have a cup of tea after dinner' Flo informed her Crewkerne friend, Miss Christopher, on this card. Looking remarkably like a Hollywood set designer's idea of an Edwardian café, Vosper Paget's elegant establishment, with its white iron arcades and marble-topped tables, added a decidedly Parisian flavour to the Bristol scene. Banquettes and Thonet chairs afforded seating while elaborately iced cakes flaunted themselves on the counter. A suitably attired gentleman represents the desired clientele. The bakers and confectioners were based in Henry Street, Totterdown, but had cafés at No. 9 Peter's Street and No. 62 West Street. The Peter's Street establishment is probably the one illustrated above. Its Georgian premises (below) stood opposite St Peter's Church and boasted an art nouveau sign advertising a 'Vegetarian Restaurant'.

CASTLE GREEN WORKS, BRISTOL.

Dangerous Neighbour

Hellier and Wills' colour manufactory faced the Castle Green Congregational Chapel and stretched back to the Frome. They were colour and oil merchants and drysalters, manufacturing white lead, colours, putty and varnish. They were originally located in Peter Street, where their warehouses stretched back to Narrow Wine Street. The combustible and toxic contents made Hellier and Co. a hazardous neighbour. On 30 March 1856, a fire quickly spread igniting 28 lbs of gunpowder stored there. The explosion shattered windows in St Peter's and the neighbourhood; four other businesses burned. By 1861 Hellier's (then called Hurndall, Hellier and Wills) were at No. 34 Castle Green. Another devastating and fatal fire started in the warehouse to the right of the entrance gateway on 4 May 1861. Paint blistered 100 yards away in the intense heat and other properties burned. Presumably the Italianate building on Ensor's 1876 trade card was then raised. After 1880 the firm was called Samuel Wills and Co.

'Them was boughten in Castle Street'

Castle Street was Bristol's bustling main shopping centre in the early 1920s. The multitude of shoppers resulted in vehicles being banned at certain times and some shops staying open until 10 p.m. to cater for customers. With its natural continuation along Old Market and surrounding streets, this was truly Bristol's commercial heart. Although blasted by the Blitz in November 1940, some shops continued trading until the 1950s. At the behest of the large chain stores, and against the protests of small traders, the council abandoned it and redeveloped Broadmead as the major shopping area. This, and the new road system, severed Old Market from shoppers, ruining its once-thriving trade. Castle Park replaced Castle Street in 1979. Remarkably, central Bristol lacked any supermarkets until the late 1980s – only the Fairfax Street Co-op and (possibly) Debenham's once included grocery departments. Otherwise Bright's upmarket food hall in Queen's Road was the only alternative for workers in need of groceries.

Dog "Punch," No. 1.

Dog Punch: The Children's Friend

From 1890, customers of Castle Street's 'The Standard of England' would soon discover landlord George Williams' engaging and well-trained dog, Punch. In all there were, successively, three dogs named Punch. Remarkably, all were trained to beg customers for coins for charity. When one was offered, Punch would then deposit the coin in a collection box at the bar. Their collection was given to the Bristol Hospital for Sick Children and Women. Punch I collected £43 9s 2½d before his death in 1894. So admired was he that the Ancient Order of Foresters had him mounted and displayed wearing his medals. His son, Punch II, collected 7,239 coins to the value of £20 18s 4½d the following year alone. So successful was this novelty that all three dogs were awarded medals for their charitable efforts. Alas, no portrait of Punch III survived the pub's destruction on 24 November 1940.

The Makers of Puritan Soap

The image shows part of Christopher Thomas & Bros Ltd's huge Italianate soap factory on Broad Plain as it appeared in 1913 on the eve of an extensive modernisation of its manufacturing and packaging processes. Bristol was historically Britain's prime manufacturer of soap and Thomas' started in Red Lion Yard, Thomas Street, in 1825. In 1841 it merged with Fry, Fripp and Co. (founded in Castle Street in 1745), becoming Christopher Thomas & Bros in 1845. By 1900 it also manufactured candles and glycerine, while its refinery produced vegetable oils for confectionary and baking. Much of the Broad Plain complex was eventually designed or remodelled by William Bruce Gingell, although other local architects such as Foster and Wood added to it. The giant soap-boiling pan building, now part of Gardiner Haskins, once boasted castellated corner-turret chimneys and a gable bell-cote. Campaniles and Italianate towers masked other chimneys on the buildings. The premises closed in the 1950s.

Welsh Back to Bristol Bridge

On Welsh Back

Tanner's Warehouse, one of Metal Agencies Co.'s premises on the corner of Crow Lane, photographed around 1935. Originally built for Tanner's manufacturing stationers, it later stored more perishable commodities and was emblazoned with the legend 'Eat more fruit and keep fit!' To the right is the City Fountain of 1859. It is hard now to appreciate how difficult it was in the past for both humans and animals to get free and pure water. By 1906 Bristol had over forty drinking fountains to ease the public's thirst. It seems probable that the 'Green City' has none working today. To the left of the warehouse was the Golden Bottle Inn, which indeed had a large golden bottle suspended outside. These properties straddled the site of the medieval St John's Chapel and also, until the late 1870s, St Nicholas' Cemetery, which was skirted by Crow Lane. The Golden Bottle (and presumably the warehouse) were lost in the Blitz.

A Floury Prospect at Buchanan's Wharf

This image shows Messrs Spillers and Bakers Ltd's impressive granary and flour mill as they appeared in 1913 after a new ferro-concrete building had been added to the assemblage on the right. William Baker built the first mill here in 1854, followed by an adjacent one in 1862. Called Redcliff Mills, the first one burned down in 1882 and was replaced in 1883 by a larger one. In 1886 a granary and silo house were added at what was then called Britannia Wharf. The buildings were converted into flats in 1988. Joel Spiller established his flour-milling business in Bridgwater in 1829. By 1832 it had expanded to Bristol and Cardiff. It became a manufacturer of ships' and later dogs' biscuits. In 1889 it became a limited company and, merging with William Baker and Sons, became Spillers and Bakers Ltd and Bristol's largest milling firm. The small building at the left was a vinegar brewery.

Grist from the Mill, 1904

'This is where the broken wheat came from and where I earn my daily bread' wrote a Spiller's miller, 'F.M.', on this card of Redcliff Back sent to Nellie Grist in 1904. Granaries and flour mill fill the left and rear of the photograph. A separate company was founded for the manufacture of biscuits and cakes, while the grain business became Spiller's Grain. Bristol had a Spiller's dog biscuit factory by 1914 and later one at Avonmouth. Modern mills designed by Oscar Faber were erected at Avonmouth for Spiller's in 1934–35 but ceased operation in 1998. Avonmouth mill and the warehouse were later demolished, leaving the derelict grain silos on the dockside. Since the 1850s at least, the buildings seen here on the right-hand side of Redcliff Back had housed Sykes and Co.'s brewery and a W. D. and H. O. Wills' tobacco factory. Domesticity has replaced milling at Buchanan's Wharf.

A Place to be Seen At, 1973

In April 1973, Ladbroke's Dragonara Hotel opened at Redcliffe Way. Its immediate attraction was The Kiln restaurant that was converted from the base of the Prewett Street glasshouse's Great Cone. Built around 1761 for Taylor's Glassworks, it originally stood over 120 feet high but had been reduced to 30 feet after 1936 when cracks appeared in the superstructure. This is the last remaining cone in a city that once boasted so many for its pottery and glassmaking industries. Ladbroke's unusual decision (for the 1970s) to convert rather than demolish gave the Dragonara something quite extraordinary in The Kiln and for celebrities and aspiring socialites, both the acclaimed restaurant and hotel soon became highly desirable institutions to be seen attending. The hotel later became part of the Ramada chain (and the restaurant converted to a carvery) but is now the DoubleTree by Hilton. The newly refurbished Kiln is known for its modern English cuisine.

So Convenient for the Railway Passenger

James B. Hemming's Terminus Hotel ('Opposite the Station'), seen here in 1859, was only one of several such minor establishments that sprung up in the vicinity of Temple Meads Station with the coming of the railway. Situated in Bath Parade (now Temple Gate), it faced the approach ramp to the joint station. Hemming was a wine merchant and his establishment offered customers a shop, refreshment and accommodation in twenty bedrooms. Foreign and British wines and spirits were on offer, although the clientele were generally not fashionable. In April 1860 James Morton, a ship's carpenter, was found hanging from a bedpost in his room. On 10 June 1861, Mr Hemming organised a special excursion train to Worcester and Birmingham to raise funds for Bristol General Hospital. On 26 June 1893, when Henry Webber was landlord, a fire devastated the ground floor and damaged the upper rooms. The hotel finally closed and was demolished in 1968–69.

The George Hotel and a lost 'triumphal arch'

The image shows the George and Railway Hotel at Temple Gate in 1956. Established before 1703 as the George and the Dragon coaching inn, it stood adjacent to the Temple Gate. Once famous for its turtle cook and 'a 120 year old paroquet', its name changed to attract clientele from the new stations. Its acquisition and rebuilding between 1868 and 1872 arose from it being in the path of the viaduct and bridge for the Bristol Harbour Railway that ultimately covered part of the old building. The new hotel included a polychrome statue of Queen Victoria on its main façade, although the proximity of the viaduct to the bedrooms can have done little to enhance the establishment in the eyes of travellers – one of Bristol's lost urinals appears to the left. The elegant columned bridge over Victoria Street was unfortunately demolished in the 1990s. Empty since 1993, and marooned by traffic schemes, a projected adjoining square may offer salvation.

'The Hotel for Business or Pleasure' Samuel Fripp's Flemish-Renaissance-style Grosvenor Hotel in Victoria Street opened in 1875. Built in red brick with Bath stone dressings, the attractive façade's main decorative feature consists of silhouetted stone reliefs, based on Flemish gables, which contrast against the brickwork. The Grosvenor's *raison d'être* was catering to railway passengers. Popular, if not fashionable, by the 1900s it promised 'an Electric Grill', a garage, and seventy rooms with hot and cold running water. A monk reputedly haunts its corridors. When owned by Claude Lloyd in the 1930s, a curving *Moderne* extension was added. Alas, the cutting of Redcliffe Way and the building of the Victoria Street flyover isolated it on a traffic island and destroyed its prosperity. In decline by the 1970s, it finally closed in the 1990s. In 1979 it featured in a Chris Petit film entitled *Radio On*. Now empty and unlisted, the building will hopefully survive.

A Modern Warehouse, 1928

Resembling a smart department store, Messrs Wilkinson and Riddell (Bristol) Ltd's warehouse stood at Nos 111–117 Victoria Street. In 1897 Bristol's wholesale textile firm of Bolt Bros was taken over by Birmingham's Wilkinson Riddell in an expansion bid. The warehouse replaced the ancient Crabb's Well inn and its neighbouring properties after their demolition in 1907. Built in a grandiose classical metropolitan style, it was eminently suitable for the wholesale draper's firm. The façade's rusticated podium was entered through a columned shell niche. Pilasters, crowned by heavily garlanded cartouches, topped the podium while pediments headed the windows of the second floor; a central pediment crowned the middle pilasters. The new building was deemed notable on account of its modern lighting system. Economical 'restoration', or modernisation, later saw the façade stripped of all classical ornamentation beyond the rustication, but it still retained a presence (photographed 2011). It was demolished early in 2016.

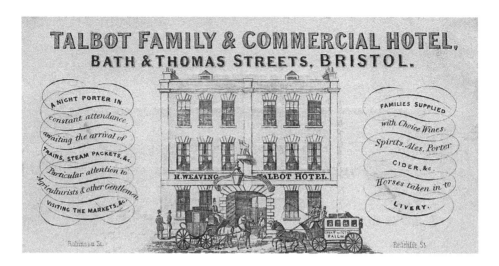

TALBOT FAMILY & COMMERCIAL HOTEL,
BATH & THOMAS STREETS, BRISTOL.

A NIGHT PORTER IN constant attendance awaiting the arrival of TRAINS, STEAM PACKETS, &c. Particular attention to Agriculturists & other Gentlemen VISITING THE MARKETS, &c.

H. WEAVING   TALBOT HOTEL.

FAMILIES SUPPLIED with Choice Wines. Spirits, Ales, Porter CIDER, &c. Horses taken in to LIVERY.

The Talbot

A carriage and a GWR omnibus arrive at the Talbot, Henry Weaving's family and commercial hotel between Bath and Thomas streets on a trade card of 1862, produced by Elisha Robinson of nearby Redcliff Street. Originally called the Pelican, and in existence before 1573, it then opened solely on to Thomas Street. Its name changed a century later and, with the cutting of Bath Street to aid access to Temple Street, William Paty's 1789 façade then matched his houses in the new thoroughfare. The Talbot was a coaching inn with a central arch through to its coach yard. Around 1873 the building of Victoria Street saw it expanded, rebuilt in polychrome brick and retitled the Royal Talbot. Positioning and its luxuriously appointed and furnished public and private rooms ensured its popularity. In 1919 Georges' Brewery purchased it for offices. Blitzed to only one storey in 1940, the façade was beautifully restored in around 1994.

'Beer is Best'

The image is an aerial view of George's Brewery in 1938 when the firm owned all buildings depicted in a darker hue. Their porter brewery had started in Tucker Street in 1788 on a site long associated with brewing, and gradually acquired adjoining properties. Tucker Street itself became the brewery's lorry and stable-yard in the 1920s when George's also acquired the Paty houses of Bath Street. At the right on the riverbank is the impressive 1930s brick-built bottling plant. Iron was originally stored in the adjoining warehouse to the left. Left again, with its boiler-house chimney, was the visually interesting Old Porter Brewery that incorporated parts of the original Georgian buildings. Its clerestory gable has survived redevelopment into the Brewhouse flats. Originally the Brew House was the striking 1920s classical building behind the Brewery now called The Tower. Georges' amalgamated with Courages in 1961. A series of takeovers followed and the brewery sadly closed in 2000.

A Brewery's Trademark, 1938

Georges' Brewery had long relied on its famous grey shire horses to deliver beer to the city's public houses. So beloved were they that the company adopted the dray horse as its trademark and the beautifully equipped shires were a familiar sight in the city streets. By the 1930s it was considered a sensible and economical way to deliver beer locally. The prize-winning horses were well looked after and the drays themselves fitted with ball-bearing wheels and pneumatic tyres to ease their burden. Georges' supplied almost a thousand houses and those further afield were served by a fleet of steam lorries (below). By 1938, the firm's 150th anniversary, petrol-driven lorries were gradually replacing the steamers. Alas, by 1961 traffic congestion and the irascibility of motorists towards the drays resulted in Georges' reluctantly deciding to dispense with the four remaining shires. All worked until good homes could be found for them.

The Other End of Bristol Bridge

'Thomas and Company wholesale and family grocery warehouse, 5 Bridge Parade, Bristol, respectfully solicit the favour of your orders', informs this business card. The delightful 1850s engraving is a rare one as it shows properties on the Redcliffe side of Bristol Bridge. On the site of Bridge Parade until the 1760s had stood the spectacular 'Great House at the Bridge End', demolished when the bridge was rebuilt. Internally Thomas' shop was long, and may have connected to a riverside warehouse at the rear. Wine merchant Thomas Clifton's riverside establishment snuggled against one of the bridge's historically notorious toll houses. The entrance to old Baldwin Street appears in the distance. Thomas' window (illuminated at night-time by six globular gasoliers) displays boxes of tea and conical sugarloafs. A shopman takes a mounted gentleman's order by the kerbside while a delivery man carries a basket of wine bottles packed in straw from Clifton's.

The Centre to Cheltenham Road

At the Garrick's Head, November 1966

Until 1979 The Garrick's Head at No. 22 Broad Quay was an architectural delight. Built in 1902 and the work of Edward Gabriel, Bristol's innovative and talented architect, like much of his work it is instilled with the spirit of the Arts and Crafts movement. The pub looked across the water at his elaborate façade for E-shed (now Watershed). The real joy of the Garrick's double-gabled and jettied façade was the pair of bow windows based on those of Sir Paul Pindar's house, preserved at the Victoria and Albert Museum. These were topped by Venetian windows below semi-annuli filled with masks and elaborate scrollwork. The pub was sandwiched between a late-Georgian shop and Tratman Bros' once elegant sailmaking establishment, unfortunately, by this time, masked in neon. After the Bristol and West Tower (now reborn as Radisson Blu) arose, their fate was sealed and they fell before that premises' expansion. Serviced apartments now cover the site.

'A gleaming white Palace of Industry'

William Venn Gough's 1905 monumental Bristol Gas Co. offices were erected on the site adjoining the Colston Hall, formerly occupied by the Salem Chapel. Between 1775 and 1830 the chapel had also held the Countess of Huntingdon Connexion (*see* page 64) before its removal to Trenchard Street. Preparatory building work uncovered part of the pipe leading to St John's Conduit via Pipe Lane. Even in 1905 Gough's brick building was old-fashioned and by 1935, to reflect the modern advances in gas cooking, it was refaced with a splendid *Moderne* façade in gleaming white Portland stone designed by Whinney, Son & Austen Hall. This glamorous showroom boasted huge shop windows displaying new gas appliances for the modern home, and doors and lifts attended by uniformed liftboys and doormen. Alas Radiant House eventually passed into city ownership and, uncared for, the façade went into visual decline. It was regrettably demolished and replaced by the tarnished gold façade to the Colston Hall's foyer.

'The finest waters in Bristol unsurpassed in clearness and brightness'
St John's Conduit in 1825 by Prout.
In 1376 the Carmelite Friars allowed St John's Parish to tap their conduit leading from springs on Brandon Hill. The fountain house stood within the gate, but was moved outside the walls in 1827–28 to allow a side arch for pedestrians to be cut. The present arrangement dates from 1866. Water flowed with few interruptions for over 600 years, surviving Bristol's 1893 fountain-closing pollution scare. During the Blitz it provided the only water source in the centre of the city. Once promoted as a historic Bristol attraction, around 2002, work in Park Street damaged the pipe. Bristol's Property Services department spent over £14,000 restoring and checking its route, via Frogmore Street and Pipe Lane. Alas, building work in Frogmore Street again severed it, but nothing has been done to locate the leak or to restore the supply. Dirty, 'tagged' and dry, the conduit today only advertises Bristol's disregard of its heritage.

The Last Days of Old Lewin's Mead

A view across Lewin's Mead Brewery from Rupert Street around 1959, looking towards the doomed properties in Lewin's Mead that redevelopment would soon sweep away. A Georgian house recalls the fact that, until the 1860s, the area had been mostly domestic with many early but decayed houses. Neat remnants of Champion's confectionery works appear on the right, backed by the Moravian school. Above these, mature trees betray the still-existing gardens of the B.R.I. Encouraged by the St James Improvement Committee, Lewin's Mead and Rupert Street were redeveloped for industry in the 1890s. By the 1960s Bristol planners (ill-inspired by thoughts of Le Corbusier) envisaged the area's pedestrians confined to walkways above the new traffic racetracks created by the inner circuit road. As official enthusiasm for the walkway scheme evaporated, speculative development was permitted to turn much of the area into urban canyons (below in October, 1971). Some redevelopment is currently underway in 2016.

'One of the city's oldest activities'

Leather factors and merchants Messrs Herbert Ashman & Co.'s impressive premises, (later the *Evening Post*'s offices), on the corner of Silver Street and Broadmead. With an abundant local water supply, so vital for the process, fellmongering and leather trading had been long established in Bristol. On 7 January 1790, a Thursday market for tanned leather was established at the Leather Hall, Welsh Back, while Wednesdays and Saturdays saw raw hides, calves skins and 'unwrought tanned leathers' sold there as well. John Thomas set up Britain's second coloured Morocco leather works at Broad Weir around 1790. Bristol became a major centre for the production and distribution of sole leather. Ashman's were founded in 1874, becoming a private limited company in 1909. With branches elsewhere in Britain, they not only traded internally but had extensive business on the Continent and throughout the colonies. Councillor, Lord Mayor and active Liberal, Sir Herbert Ashman became a Baronet in 1907.

'The Genuine English Tradesman'

The image shows Broadmead before pedestrianisation around 1968. More properties than those blitzed were demolished to achieve the post-war shopping development. Woolworth's 1950–52 fin-clad façade replaced temporary accommodation at its bombed 1911 Castle Street store. In 1982 Broadmead's Woolworth was chosen for an experiment in attracting young professionals and was renamed '21st Century Shopping'. Its enhanced and altered ranges included groceries and plants among the innovations. This author found it an improvement, but it was not sufficiently successful for the owners. Renamed 'Woolworth's' in 1983, it fell before the Galleries project in 1988. Until 1833 the house and fellmongering works of John Narraway, the host of the ultimately remarkably inconsiderate teenage artist Turner, occupied Woolworth's and the Galleries' site. Fascinating Narraway correspondence discovered by the author is published in his volume *Bristol in 1807*. Although terminally ill, in 1822 the kindly, well-respected Narraway attempted to stop a cruel bear and badger baiting event from being held in a Broadmead loft.

'Cupids standing on one leg with extended pinions'

In 1864 the confectioner Mr Jerman started a new business at No. 4 Lewin's Mead. By 1885, under the ownership of his erstwhile manager Robert Champion, it had become the world's largest steam confectionery works. Rebuilt following a devastating fire in 1890, the works became 'an island with sides facing Lewin's Mead, Maudlin St, Deep St and Gravel St'. Robert died in 1895 and was commemorated in St James' Church in 1896 by a wrought-iron chancel screen designed by Stacy of Baldwin Street. Champions produced every sort of confectionery in a multitude of shapes and packaging for a worldwide market. Wartime damage saw the firm move to St Werburgh's; it closed around 1962. The 1961 photograph, taken from Lewis' roof garden, shows the partially gutted factory (foreground). Behind the Eye Hospital on the right, the arcaded windows of the Moravian school in Blackfriars appear. On the left, Bristol's first multistorey car park of 1960, designed by Jelinek-Karl, protrudes.

Swings and Roundabouts

A fair occupies the Hay Market in 1880. On the right runs the Horse Fair while to the left St James' burial ground and Bond Street (once Barton Alley) appears. The latter runs to St James' Barton and thence to Stokes Croft. Its gabled national school buildings ('serving the lowest of the low') and neighbouring properties fell before the new bus station in the 1950s. In 1878 St James parish reportedly had at least fifty brothels – three close to the school. In the left distance towers Derham's boot factory and to its right 'The Barton', Cordeux's linen drapers. The picturesque jumble of buildings in St James' Churchyard at the rear of the fair is dominated by the polychrome-brick façade of the recently rebuilt and expanded eleven-room Rose & Crown. Behind them ran the Upper Arcade. The pub was renamed the White Lion in 1891. It was demolished for Lewis's department store around 1953 along with two other hostelries.

The Wonder of Traffic Circulatory Systems (part one)

Teenagers Jackie Sobey and Alan Anstee snapped by a commercial street photographer in St James' Barton in 1959. They stand on the corner of Barr's Street, which would now be above the centre of the 'Bear Pit' underpass. Behind them are buildings in North Street, Stokes Croft, soon doomed to fall before the onslaught of redevelopment. Behind Alan, 'The Window Box', was Potts and Harveys' ladies outfitters at No. 2 North Street. Opposite it, Georgian buildings adjoining the Full Moon inn appear. By 1968 all but one of these buildings had been swept away for the first stage of Bristol's traffic circulatory system that would eventually develop into the present St James' Barton roundabout. Three police officers direct traffic through a scene of desolation (below). Cumberland Street appears to the right. In 1969 construction started on the monolithic road-spanning horror of Avon House North (since 2001, '51.02 Apartments') and adjoining Barton and York Houses.

Welcome to Babyland

The proud proprietor of the Bristol Pram Co., perambulator manufacturers, stands outside his newly opened shop at No. 3 King Square Avenue in 1926. Before 1950s redevelopment the premises lay on the avenue's turning into North Street (approximately where the parked car stands on the left of the modern photograph) and hoped to benefit from the passing trade into Stokes Croft. Artistic window dressing was not a company skill as is all too obvious. Alas, the venture failed and by 1929 Robert Trevis' fancy goods occupied the building. The avenue had been planned in the 1740s to connect King Square (originally New Square) with the city. Its buildings included a terrace north of Charles Street and some simple but elegant late Georgian commercial façades to the south. Only Nos 11 and 9 now remain, the latter camouflaged by local artists 3Dom and Haka's freehand spray-paint mural of 2011.

Problems with Progress

A corporation water cart lays road dust in Stokes Croft around 1895. A country-town-type high street and a prosperous, although not fashionable, shopping area. On the right the regrettably lost, elegant twin-winged façades of Stokes Croft School and almshouses founded in a semi-rural area in 1722 by the Lewin's Mead Meeting. The almshouses occupied the wings, the school the centre. Horfield Steam Tramway Co.'s introduction of steam trams to the road in 1880 frightened horses and caused great annoyance to local shopkeepers, who sent a deputation to the Corporation. In narrow North Road their presence was particularly alarming. Apart from the vehicles' unaccustomed rattling, young drivers delighted in constantly blowing the whistles. Damaged in the Blitz, Stokes Croft and St James Barton, like Old Market, were economically blighted by Bristol's post-war traffic schemes that unnaturally isolated them from Broadmead's shoppers, 'Perpetuating the emptiness of devastation by building another of their roundabouts,' observed Nikolaus Pevsner in 1958.

'Situated very near the fields'
Daniel Asher Alexander's Baptist Academy in Stokes Croft in 1967. The college for training ministers originated in Barr Street in the eighteenth century but, between 1806 and 1812, a new £12,000 building arose at Stokes Croft close to the city boundary. Behind it a considerable offshoot of Miller's Nursery, bounded by what are now City and Ashley roads, stretched as far as Albert Place. A nobly severe, classical building, the Academy would later be likened to a prison or a workhouse, and possibly its design inspired some of Bristol's later warehouses. The entrance arch adjoined the Principal's substantial house with its pedimented and rusticated central doorway. In 1919 the college moved to Tyndall's Park, close to the university and the Western College. By 1967 the old building was a Christian Science church. A doorway had replaced one of its front windows, chimneys removed, and the roof was of corrugated sheeting. It was unfortunately demolished in 1972.

Long May He Reign!

In top hat and frock coat, banker Edward Sargent joins the staff of Stokes Croft's branch of the National Provincial Bank preparing for the local celebrations marking the Coronation of Edward VII in 1902. Shields and flags decorate the façade and wooden shuttering protects the windows from the expected crowds, foiling attempts to stand on window ledges. Flags were commonly used for celebratory decoration. Georgian visitors enthused over Bristol's custom of studding the outsides of their church towers with them. The wall by the young girl standing in Hepburn Road (originally Adams Court) bears graffiti in the days when this consisted of chalk drawings. In this case someone has been practising their letters and drawing window frames. The Bank (No. 84 and now a bar/restaurant called the Love Inn), was built in the front garden of the elegant double-bowed Georgian Stokes Croft House that continued to function behind as a club.

'Taking pride and delight in all his work'
William Wilmut (1847–1911), architectural sculptor and woodcarver of No. 7 Picton Street, Stokes Croft, among members of his staff around 1896. His sons William Edwin (1873–1938) and Albert (1874–*c.* 1936) were woodcarvers and masons respectively. William Snr stands fifth from the left and William Jnr third from right. The firm moved to Picton Street (below) in 1893, where William also taught woodcarving. Wilmut's work appears all over the West Country. In Bristol his many commissions included the teak altar in the Lord Mayor's Chapel, panels in the Bishop's Palace and 'the new tower' at Clifton College. He produced staircases and pews and even doors for London's National Gallery. Restoration work included the ancient bench ends at Mullion in Cornwall. The family lived at No. 133 Ashley Road and Wilmut was choirmaster at St Agnes Church for seven years, from its consecration in 1886. He produced the screen and all the woodcarvings in that church.

'For the District and adjacent Horfield'

A clamour for branch libraries followed Bristol's adoption of the Public Libraries Act in 1874. St Philips was the first in 1876, followed in March 1877 by St James (later North District) occupying No. 26 King Square. By 1898 this was inadequate and William Venn Gough won the commission for a new (somewhat old-fashioned) building on a previously domestic site on the Cheltenham Road. The brick and Bath-stone building opened in 1901 and included a library bindery at the rear (below in 1960). This department saved Bristol thousands of pounds in rebinding and recycling its book-stock, but closed in the early 1990s as an economy measure. Henceforth, the service could only afford to commercially bind periodicals, and books were thereafter withdrawn once well-used. The library burned in the Blitz and was reduced in size, being renamed 'Cheltenham Road' after the 1970s. There are plans to relocate the branch to the Gloucester Road.

Around College Green

Sacrilege! When Stonehenge Came to College Green

On Saturday 18 August 2012 Bristolians were surprised to experience the surreal sight of the centre of College Green occupied by a bouncy castle in the form of a life-size inflatable copy of Stonehenge. Jeremy Deller's art installation 'Sacrilege' was a co-commission between Glasgow International Festival of Visual Art and the Mayor of London, with support from Arts Council England. It travelled to twenty-six locations around the UK as part of the London 2012 Festival. Its light-hearted intention was to induce people of all ages to think about one of the UK's most iconic historic monuments while inducing a sense of play. The juxtapositioning of an important pagan building next to a Christian one added a new dimension to the installation in Bristol. The photograph below shows the same view in 1935, when the 1851 replica of Bristol's High Cross still reigned over the paths and lawns of the Green.

'Gimcrack stucco work, gilded incongruities'

In 1778 St Mark's Chapel on College Green was given a Gothic portico. In 1822 the chapel, 'having been again allowed to fall into ignorant and presumptive hands', was the subject of a seven-year restoration programme. Repairs were undertaken by sculptor-cum-stonemason Thomas Clarke, who also replaced the great west window overlooking the Green. The original was given to Mr Cave of Henbury Hill House. In 1823 'City Painter' William Edkins was employed to design a new gallery for the chapel. The following year, with Thomas Garrard, 'City Chamberlain and collector of curiosities', they commenced collecting old stained glass and produced an antechamber to the chapel costing £1,400 in a highly polychromatic theatrical Gothic style (photographed 1880). This 'paltry gingerbread work' proved an anathema to late Victorian sensibilities: 'wooden columns and much vaulting, a mass of lathes and plaster ... gold and coloured in execrable taste'. Both antechamber and porch were removed in 1889.

When Camelot Came to College Green

In 1904 La Trobe and Weston's artistic premises for estate agent Walter Hughes opened at No. 80 College Green. Its façade and interior incorporated the work and ideas of Hughes' artistic daughter Catherine, whose studio was above the cathedral archway. Her second-floor mosaic panel and the flanking copper window hoods bear symbolic pomegranates. Walter's offices were fronted by his favourite polished red granite. A column divided the matching doors leading to the upper floors and adjoining No. 80A, the new extension to Percy Gane's furnishing gallery. Café entrepreneur P. J. Lloyd developed the upper floors into the artistic Cabot Café. Its first floor held the 55-foot-long Cabot Room. Its wainscoted walls were topped by Bristolian William Arthur Chase's six-panel frieze depicting John Cabot's voyage. The second floor held the green-clad Camelot Room. Here, copper strips divided five Chase depictions of King Arthur's tale. Modernised as a Cadena Café in 1932, it was damaged in the Blitz that destroyed its neighbours.

'Advanced suffragistic ideals'

Staff surround city librarian E. R. Norris Mathews and his deputy, Launcelot Acland Taylor, at the new central library's opening in 1906. Bristol pioneered the employment of female librarians 'of good education and respectable parentage' when it was frowned upon elsewhere – applicants first sat an examination and might wait four years for a position. Bristol also pioneered a hierarchical approach to the profession for females, with staff graded by titles. None could marry however, and because they had 'less in the way of personal expenses or worldly responsibilities', all were paid less than their male colleagues. Men worked behind the scenes and both sexes were kept apart at breaks. Inevitably conflict arose during the era of the suffragette, especially during the First World War, eventually resulting in pay rises. Below, the author (second right) and colleagues don costume in 2009 for a cultural evening launching the library's N.L.F. funded volume *Bristol in 1807*, a permanent record of the 1807 exhibition.

'Thou shalt not covet thy neighbour's house', 1957 and 2013

Bristolians own their city's book-stock and librarians are there to exploit and protect it for future generations. In 2013 it was expected that the council would celebrate its library's quadricentennial anniversary; instead it announced that it favoured an approach by Bristol Cathedral School to form a primary school in the library's lower floors. Notwithstanding informed public protest, the request was granted. The building-wide stacks held bound periodicals, rare and valuable collections, and the reserve lending and art book-stock used daily to make the service function. Some book-stock was accommodated on-site after 'weeding', but periodicals and rarer volumes were banished to Hotwells for weekly retrieval, much to the detriment of researchers and an increasingly busy service. Archival and bound local newspapers, devoid of special shelving, languish on floors in another conservationally-unfriendly warehouse with a 'non-use' directive. A library's usefulness depends on librarians' personal knowledge of its book-stock and content, accumulated by daily familiarity, which cannot be fully achieved when books are located elsewhere.

'A place belonging to them, so pleasing and so suitable'

Tyndale Church Mission (photographed 1908) opened in a Lamb Street cottage in 1870 in what was then 'a needy district'. Flourishing, they spread to the 'old Jews' synagogue' and Cromwell's House in Lower College Green and a disused pub, the 'House of Rest', ending up occupying four properties. Securing a site adjoining the Deanery Road Viaduct, Foster and La Trobe's £2,600, purpose-built, three-storey Flemish-style building opened in 1888. It catered for the social, cultural, educational, sporting and religious needs of its congregation, even providing winter playrooms for children. The stone-built ground floor on Lamb Street housed classrooms for juniors and infants, while the middle brick-built floor had rooms for senior scholars. The Deanery Road floor held a large hall. In 1919 the Mission evolved to become the Folk House but was extensively damaged on 2 December 1940 in an incendiary raid. Restored, it was finally demolished in 1964 (below) for the new extension to the Central Library.

The Lost Deanery

The L-shaped residence of the Deans of Bristol (anciently called the Dove House) occupied the western edge of College Green's plateau. Its dormitory ceilings bore remarkable Elizabethan allegorical paintings that are now in the cathedral. Dean Creswick restored the deanery in 1734 and William Warburton virtually rebuilt it in 1758. One Bath-stone wing with a rusticated ground floor stretched across to where the Council House stands today; a garden lay behind. Unity Street then ran past its pierced area balustrade and through the arch. When Revd John Lamb died in 1850, 300 bottles of wine were in the cellars. The latter may partially survive as the library's legendary 'lost room' beneath the road as several circular skylights are still visible in that building's 'moat'. Occupied by the Y.W.C.A from 1861, it was demolished for the building of Deanery Road in 1865 and the Central Library in 1902. The author's reconstruction is based on Georgian sketches.

'A Goddess of Sex'

In 1939 Alfred Hardiman was commissioned to provide stone sculptures and bronze unicorns to flank the new Council House's central doorway. Although the unicorns were cast, the council broke the contract in 1942 without fully reimbursing Hardiman. A new contract commissioned two 30-foot-high bronze fountain sculptures of Night (*Nyx*) and Day (*Hemera*). In 1945 the Royal Academy exhibited the much-admired, half-scale maquette of Nyx. Alas, its archaic-modernist nudity caused a furore among Bristol's prudes and Christians. Newspaper correspondence reminded Bristolians of the fate of Rome and Sodom – the cathedral called it 'unsettling'. Supporters scattered the prudes but the damage was done. Inter-departmental confusion resulted in the council refusing payment, denying the contract existed. Hardiman died in 1949, unpaid, and knowing David McFall was then sculpting new unicorns. Mrs Hardiman's pleas for payment were unpleasantly ignored. Nyx was displayed at London's Festival of Britain and then accepted into Aberdeen Art Gallery's collection (below). Storage subsequently destroyed it.

Two Entrepreneurs and a Hotel

College Green was anciently known as Billeswick or 'beautiful place'. This photograph from 1928 of its western side features the Elizabethan- or Jacobean-gabled building that was its earliest surviving house, then occupied by the Bristol Education Committee's West Bristol clinic. Adjoining it, the huge studio windows of Joseph Bell's stained-glass workshops appear. Internationally admired, Bell produced glass at College Green from 1858. In the foreground Bryan Brother's Cathedral, or Royal Garage, occupied the garden once alongside the demolished Deanery. James Bryan's remarkable career encompassed errand boy, barrow boy, waiter and taxi driver. Starting his own firm in Boar's Head Yard, he later opened a car dealership on College Green. Bryan Brothers prospered and still survives. The Cathedral Hotel, 'replete with all the comforts of home', occupied two Georgian houses. Adjoining were Bristol's Gas Meter Testing office and an annexe to the Colston Hall. All were demolished in 1933 for the proposed new Council House.

The Prospect from the Leads

Canon's Marsh seen from the roof of the Central Library's 1966 extension in June 1973 contrasted with February 2016 (taken from the Holden building). Lower Lamb Street points towards the gasworks, ruined engine sheds and adjacent car park. It is flanked on the left by the workshops of Rowe's metal windows and Bristol Wool and on the right by the extensive premises of Bryan Brothers Motor Engineers of Deanery Road. To the right of the distant bonded warehouses rises the white, pillar-like sign of the Cathedral Garage in St George's Road. Redevelopment has seen domestic occupation replace Bryan Brothers, and the Cathedral School's expansion has claimed Rowe's and what had been the library's staff garden and furniture stores. A bright yet mostly disappointing, cluttered and seemingly unplanned melange of banal architecture now occupies the prospect. The unfinished windows to the right of the white library chimney betray the absence of the extension's planned upper storey.

A Return to Domesticity

The Council House and the 1869 Deanery Road Viaduct now cover the original Lamb Street. An adjoining road to its south called Bishop's Park (recalling the predecessor of the Georgian estate) was renamed Lower Lamb Street. The artisan houses of Trinity Row, Stephens' Court and Park Square lay on its eastern side, while beyond were the larger houses forming the western side of Lower College Green. Many survived until the 1930s, although Rowe's workshop replaced Trinity Row. The Blitz of 1940 destroyed more including those on Lower College Green. In 1950 the council acquired the triangle of land on the east side of the street, intending eventually to build an extension to the Central Library. Bryan Brothers acquired the western side, now rebuilt as flats. The 1973 photograph shows the post-war workshops. Alas, an expiring Avon County Council sold the land that now houses student accommodation and an extension to the Cathedral School.

'Where once there were cottages'. Anchor Road, 1965

From 1770 the new Park Estate developed on Bishop's Park, west of College Green's plateau. Both photographs are taken from the centre of what was once Park Square. Originally Anchor Lane ran further south, bounding the rope-walk sheds that stretched from the present Travelodge to beyond Millennium Square. The evolution of Canons Marsh from sawmills and marble yards into a railway goods depot and warehousing removed housing but also necessitated the provision of a better approach road. The new 1890s Anchor Road removed historic buildings on the southern side of Lower or Inner College Green (now College Square) and those to the east and west. On the left, the trees once masked a public lavatory known as a notorious 'cottage', which was often visited (in a professional capacity) by the police. Currently plans to improve the square and College Green are under consideration. A sterile glass wall now mostly flanks the road on the right.

The Timber Yards of Canon's Marsh

A watercolour by the Revd John Eden (1766–1840) of Sea Banks around 1820, looking across Canon's Marsh to the unrestored cathedral. Fenced timber yards then occupied the area, while right of centre, what would become Canon's Marsh Road runs between the angled sheds. Far right are shipyards on the site of the later Liverpool Wharf. The surprisingly bosky nature of the terrain is partly accounted for by the tree-lined drainage ditch that crossed the marsh together with gardens and allotments linked to the scatter of houses. Below the cathedral was an historic rope-walk, once also fringed by avenues of trees. The red roofs of Trinity Street appear right of the cathedral. Today this prospect is filled by the Arup Associates' 1988–94 postmodern 'banana' and 'doughnut' headquarters buildings belonging to Lloyds TSB. This watercolour has hung in the office formerly used by the city librarian since 1906.

From Trenchard Street to 'Clovelly'

In Trenchard Street, 1965

Demolition claims the buildings on Stoney Hill above Trenchard Street in preparation for the construction of the Trenchard Street car park. It will soon remove Thomas Paty's houses of the 1780s on the south side of Lodge Street as well. Dominating the scene is the handsome Trenchard or Lodge Street Chapel, itself demolished in May 1967. The attractive building was built in 1830–31 in a style between Gothic and classical for the Countess of Huntingdon's Connexion. The chapel could seat 800 worshippers at its biweekly services. It was sold in 1911 and became Rankin Brothers' printing works. During demolition some thirty coffins were discovered in a crypt under the chapel. The polygonal apse and Bath-stone gable of the chapel appear above the roof of the Salem Chapel, now the site of the Colston Hall's new foyer on E. Dudley Smith's photograph taken from St Stephen's Tower in 1864.

When My Ship Comes In

Loxton's 1905 recording of Kent's Buildings looking towards Park Row from Orchard Street. The Shepherd's Arms in Frogmore Street appears far right. Kent's Buildings was typical of the numerous courts and alleys that clung to the hillside in this island of Georgian (and earlier) properties. Houses in Wells and Culver streets showed more architectural pretension. The former sported bays below Venetian windows. The area had declined socially by 1900 and, with its proximity to the port, had become well known for prostitution. Central Library staff were surprised at the level of interest that some women took in *Lloyd's List's* shipping intelligence until it was realised that they were looking for clientele among the newly docked vessels. 'Business' generally took place standing in doorways. American forces selflessly boosted profits in the 1940s. 'We counted seventeen condoms in one lane alone one Monday morning when going up to lunch in Park Row' an elderly female librarian recalled.

Bristol: Entertainment Capital of the South West

In 1966 the largest entertainment complex in Europe, Mecca's 'New Bristol Centre', opened in Frogmore Street. Costing £2 million, it contained an ice rink, bowling alleys, the Locarno Ballroom (capable of holding more than 2,000 dancers), The Craywood Club casino, a nightclub, bars, a huge cinema and a multistorey car park. The dozen bars were themed with names such as Bali Hai (complete with plastic palms and hostesses in grass skirts), Le Club or the Victorian Bar. The ABC Cinema itself cost £100,000 and was one of the last to boast a huge screen and single auditorium. Mecca added an ice hockey arena to its rink in 1981. Alas, the huge venture gradually foundered. In 1980 the cinema was divided into two units that eventually closed. Parts of the complex became the inevitable students' flats. In 2012 the dilapidated, but still popular, ice rink closed.

St George's Road, 1971

St George's Road was once known as Museum Avenue on account of the Philosophical Institution on the corner of Park Street that became Bristol's first museum and later the Freemasons' Hall. On the left the Mauretania, with its roof garden, replaced Hanmer's Buildings in 1938. Originally Museum Avenue terminated at the junction with Hill Street and a building stretched across what is now road. In 1909 a new Arts and Crafts-style Blind Asylum Workshop replaced it. Beyond was the Boars Head inn's yard. The workshop building was truncated in the 1930s when the road was cut through to join St George's Road. The remaining section was plainly refaced in brick with Crittall windows. One of its earlier windows survived at the corner of Hill Street. What had been part of Boars Head's yard appears between their two buildings. Dreary car parks and Cabot House appear distantly, replacing Georgian College Street. Dean's Court postgraduate student accommodation had replaced the workshops by 2001.

'Not a mere pleasure resort, but excellent for invalids', 1903

After the rigours of the Turkish bath, a plashing fountain together with windows and stalls embellished with painted glass featuring waterfowl and boats aided customer relaxation in the Cooling Room at the Hydro in College Place, St George's Road. Rugs ornamented the tiled floor. Once Brunel's Royal Western Hotel, the grand establishment reopened as Bartholomew's Turkish Bath in 1855 and survived as a hydro until the 1950s. Later demolition retained the façade and in 1982 it opened as council offices, renamed Brunel House. The building appears below in 1969. To its right the Edwardian Blind Workshops appears with its 1936 utilitarian frontage that was not without its admirers when demolished in 1993. Trees on the hillside beyond, once in the gardens of the Baillie House and then the bombed Prince's Theatre, show where flats would soon rise. To their right the AA offices (now the Panoramic flats), would soon replace the large Victorian buildings.

Messrs J. Fuller's Coach Factory, Bristol

On 3 June 1890 fire consumed John Fuller's three-storey carriage showrooms in St George's Road. £10,000 worth of damage was done with 150 carriages lost. Fortunately the adjoining Grindell and Kent's horse repository was saved, as were surrounding houses in College Street. Fuller's carriage works opposite were not damaged. These stood on the site of Brandon Court and were bordered by the steps of Devil's Alley (now, prosaically, Brandon Steps). Fuller decided to rebuild the undamaged works and employed Edward Gabriel, who designed a five-gable, four-storey building for him. Decoration incorporating heraldry and Fuller's initials filled each gable. The grid-like façade bore Ipswich windows and a corner tower that was a precursor of Gabriel's 1894 E-Shed design. Each floor represented one stage in carriage assembly. An extension was added by the 1900s. Needlessly demolished in 1971, the untidy site became a car park for decades. Canard Court (seen under construction below in 2008) replaced it.

A Hidden Viaduct

Originally the route to Hotwells from Bristol was via Lime Kiln Lane (now St George's Road). This 1957 aerial photograph taken after bombing and the first demolitions of the Park Estate behind the Council House illustrates how the 1869 viaduct carrying Deanery Road up to the College Green plateau at rooftop level brutally dissected the Georgian estate. Adjoining the library on the right is the Tyndale Mission and the remnants of original cottages of Lower College Green. In the foreground the gasworks, the marshalling yard and Anchor Road appear. The tall block of 1870s shops in Deanery Road and Brandon Street were soon supplanted by the ugly brick bulk of Cabot House. The post-demolition site of the latter appears below on 2 October 2008 following archaeological excavation. Looking south, the viaduct wall appears and at the left the artificial ramp of College Street rises. Crenellations on the library's extension mark the windows of its unbuilt storey.

A Different Sort of 'Local', 4 April 1908
Dr Richard Glover of Tyndale
Baptist Church stands at the door of
St George's Road Men's Club and Lad's
Institute. The road was considered a
more respectable street in what had, by
the 1880s, become a slum area, 'a sink
into which had drained some of the
city's dregs'. Poverty, filth, drunkenness,
ignorance and starvation abounded in
the once-elegant houses that were now
under multi-occupation. The area's only
benefit was that it was removed from
the stench of the harbour. Thomas
Howe, the first Tyndale Missioner,
worked tirelessly to improve the
inhabitants' lot. Gradually emphasis
shifted to education and the College
Green Men's Club Adult School was
based here at No. 88. Beyond food
and temperance beverages, the Club
offered billiards, a chess club, reading
room and a sickness benefit scheme.
From these activities evolved the Folk
House, an independent adult education
institution. The City of Bristol College
now occupies the site.

Women and Children Only!

The Read Dispensary for Women and Children (recorded here in 1907 by Samuel Loxton) was established in 1874 to allow women to consult female doctors, which were then still a novelty. Apart from Sundays, it opened daily for the admission of patients between 11.30 and 12.30. Voluntary subscriptions and patients' payments funded it. Its medical staff were from the all-female Bristol Private Hospital for Women and Children in Berkeley Square. Although for a while housed in temporary accommodation at No. 76 St George's Road, in 1905 a peninsular of land was obtained at the confluence with Anchor Road, where a drastic widening of the latter opposite the gasworks had seen the demolition of a Methodist chapel and other buildings. J. P. Sturge & Sons' Arts and Crafts-style dispensary was raised at a cost of £2,800. In 1907, 2,755 patients from Bristol and beyond visited it a total of 10,728 times.

'Ornamental to the district although not unnecessarily ornamental'

In 1833 a Methodist chapel arose at the corner of Hotwell Road and Wood-Well Lane, which later became the Church of St Peter, Cliftonwood. By 1878 the parish's 4,000 mostly humble inhabitants had outgrown it. With the demolition of Lambwell Court, adjoining land was obtained next to World's End Lane and the foundation stone laid in September 1878. The architects were Vincent William Voisey (1845–1891) and Frank William Wills (1852–1932), who had designed the 1875 Union Chapel at Portishead. The partnership was dissolved in October 1881 before the consecration in September 1882. Their St Peter's was 'Very chaste and pleasing early Gothic'. It cost over £8,000, seated 1,000 and was orientated north–south with an apsidal chancel. The tower led to a southern gallery but never received its 160-foot octagonal spire. The original church became Hotwells' Branch Library. St Peter's was demolished in 1938 and replaced by the council flats that covered both churches in the 1950s.

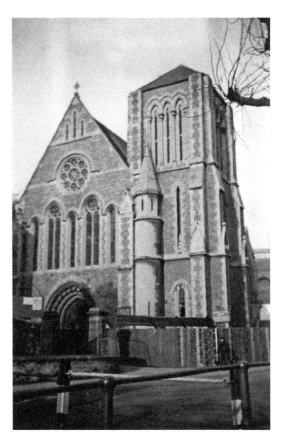

the House built by
Hippisley - where in after
and lived his daughter ...

Theatre, Water and Ecclesiastical Land-Grabbing

London actor John Hippisley opened the Jacob's Well Theatre in 1729 behind his house at the far left. Hippisley's daughter, Mrs Green, later resided there. Notwithstanding the theatre's size, (actors exiting from one wing circled the rear of the building to gain the other), it was very successful. Next door was the King William IV, with landlady Elizabeth Dawe's name appearing on its sign. Georgian baths for fashionable cold-bathing appear to the right. The spring was traditionally connected with Bristol's medieval Jewry. Pipes (replaced in iron in 1864) supplied subscribers around College Green. In 1888 Bristol Cathedral offered the (by now suspect) waters for Jacob's Well Baths. Connection would cost Bristol £840 and the clerics also requested the land between the cathedral and the Norman Gateway in return. Councillors willingly gave it, notwithstanding one vociferous accusation of ecclesiastical land-grabbing. Dr Robert Bartley's 1842 recording is from Richard Smith's collection of theatrical memorabilia in the Bristol Reference Library.

'The Clovelly of Bristol'

Rock Court was a quiet Georgian cul-de-sac off of Berkeley Place nestling against the hillside that had suggested its name. Its fourteen identical houses were linked by flights of steps where the gradient was steepest. With three storeys and deep cellars, they formed a charming example of a Georgian artisan housing development. Described as 'desirable' in an 1885 advertisement, each house had six rooms and a backyard. Unfortunately, in the mid-1960s the Queen's Road Association of Shopkeepers petitioned the council for more car-parking in the area to attract motorists to their shops. The council's solution (and not one that the Association desired), was to demolish not only the houses of Rock Court but also those of Burton and Berkeley Courts on either side of it. Demolition started in April 1966. West End multistorey car park now occupies the site.

From Marlborough Street to 'Sweden'

In Marlborough Street, 1905

Originally Lower and Upper Maudlin lanes (now streets) carried traffic from The Haymarket to St Michael's Hill and, somewhat circuitously, to Clifton. Widened after 1868, it facilitated access to the new Perry Road. The old route was partly immortalised by tramlines and here in 1904 a tramcar emerges from Lower Maudlin Street by the side of Thomas Paty's 1784 infirmary. Facing it in Marlborough Street were a motley collection of Georgian and refaced earlier properties that were demolished by 1910 to make way for Charles Holden's new hospital building and its gardens. What sculptural decoration Holden deemed necessary for his hospital mostly occurred on this southern entrance front, consisting of monumental inscriptions, unlit and flaming torches (symbolising life, the regenerative power of the flame and learning) and *paterae*. Until Jamaica Street was extended around 1869, any access to Stokes Croft from Marlborough Street was via Hillgrove Street.

'The Finest Operating Theatres in Europe'

Charles's Holden's King Edward VII Memorial Building (Bristol Royal Infirmary) of 1911–12 has long been masked by later hospital expansion. Founded in 1735, the first building was replaced in 1784. By 1910 this was dealing with 61,000 patients a year and expansion was vital. The new Portland-stone building housed surgical, casualty and specialist departments and accommodated 181 patients. Shaped like an 'E', it faced west with three separate blocks joined by bridge corridors. Triple-aspect wards were flooded with daylight and floors and ceilings curved where they joined walls to prevent dirt gathering. Terraced on a hillside, one wing was higher than the other, but the columned loggias masked this from the road. Holden replaced an existing street crossing the site with a monumental flight of steps. Relying on the decorative effects of light and shade, he employed a minimum of sculptural decoration. His arched chimneys referred to a detail of the old B.R.I. building's architecture.

Bristol Royal Infirmary, King Edward VII. Memorial.
COPYRIGHT, BURGESS & CO.   3001

'An El Dorado for the Botanist Patient!'

Holden's remarkable new hospital included one aspect of healing that has long been erased from the site: it was set in beautiful gardens. The practice of pushing patients' beds out into the gardens for fresh air and sunshine had been an important element of treatment developed in the old Infirmary. The new building boasted loggias and roof gardens to permit easy access to fresh air. Its 2-acre gardens were designed by W. E. Budgett and included flower beds, trellises, specimen trees and shrubs, many of which were donated by such contemporary gardeners as Canon Ellacombe. Their purpose was to bring health and pleasure to patients and staff. The terraced Broad Walk linked the hospital with the nurses' home (below, right) and accessed more hillside gardens above. A nursery was established for renewal. Alas, the famed rose beds, lawns, trellises and 'quiet nooks' raved about by the press have vanished under post-war hospital expansion.

At Home with the Allis Family

Around 1864 teenager Edward Hagger Allis (1849–1911) took the above photograph of his mother Caroline and young sister Florence sitting outside of the garden door at Rupert House, No. 2 Lower Church Lane. Their impressive four-storey house was by St Michael's Church and next to the rectory. It filled the area between Upper and Lower Church Lanes where St Michael on the Mount School's circular garden is now. Edward and his father John Hagger Allis were watchmakers. Edward's photograph grouped together various garden ornaments interspersed with gardening implements along the central path. A less cluttered garden appears in the photograph of 1870, taken by Caroline's father, John Sebry. The family enjoy fruitcake and sherry on the lawn. The garden door seen in the upper photograph appears left of the bow and a conservatory stands to the right. John Hagger Allis died that year aged fifty-three.

The Prospect from Rupert House, 1865

The air's clarity and lack of smoke suggest that it is Sunday. St John's, Christ Church and All Saints' dominate as yet unchallenged by the bulk of the Grand Hotel of 1864–89. On the hillside below Lower Church Lane most properties await demolition for the new link-road. Here stood Prospect House Academy, founded in 1800 and for forty-three years the favourite institute for the sons of Bristol's elite. Edward Allis' photograph shows the unroofed walls of one of its deserted classrooms. The complex and playground appear on an invitation to a 'Rehearsal of the Young Gentlemen' in 1801. George Pocock (1774–1843), its wonderfully eccentric headmaster, invented a boy-spanking machine. Being a devotee of kites and wind power, he also invented the 'Charvolant' or kite-powered carriage, taking both his family and horse to Marlborough for the day on one occasion. An adjoining house, Odd Fellows' Arms, dated 1670, together with the historic 'Bristol Steps', were also among the doomed antiquities.

Perry Road: 'One of the handsomest thoroughfares'

On 20 August 1868 Bristol celebrated the opening of the new easy-gradient link road facilitating access to Clifton and Redland from Maudlin Street and Stokes Croft. Commencing at the King David Inn and ending at the Red Lodge, it formed the base of a triangle with two roads (Griffin Lane and Lower St Michael's Hill) running from Christmas Steps. Designed by Frederick Ashmead and built at a cost of £13,302, it was named after John Perry, chairman of the Board of Health. The great difficulty faced was the construction of the massive terracing walls on the steep hillside. The new road was 50 feet wide with nine foot pavements. Its construction swept away much that was historic in St Michael's. In September 1867 the houses separating Griffin Lane and Lower Church Lane (seen here in Samuel Loxton's recording) were demolished. Park Row was similarly widened from June 1867 and later Maudlin Street to the infirmary.

'The elegantly decorated Temple of the Muses', 1870

The New Theatre Royal opened in Park Row on 14 October 1867, replacing the Baillie family's house and gardens where Queen Charlotte had once stayed. Commissioned from the theatre architect C. J. Phipps by J. H. Chute of the Theatre Royal, King Street, it rose in six months at a cost of £17,000. The builders were Davis and Sons. This early photograph shows it before a canopy was attached to its façade and four statues added to its entablature. Tattered posters on the adjoining vacant lot advertise a performance by Mary Scott Siddons, great granddaughter of Sarah. An adjoining commercial terrace identical to that already constructed would soon be added here. Notwithstanding praiseworthy safety features to allow speedy exit in the event of fire, on 27 December 1869 eighteen people, mostly teenagers, were crushed to death in a corridor while 2,000 people were attempting to enter the building. The theatre aggrandised the newly widened Park Row.

‘This well-equipped theatre in Park Row’

On the 4 August 1884 the New Theatre Royal, by then Bristol's major touring venue, was officially renamed the Prince's Theatre. Five years later it closed for over a month for alterations to be made by theatre architect Frank Matcham. It was then also redecorated by the Plastic Decoration Co., a famous London firm of decorative plasterers. Their work appears here in the theatre's splendid Grand Lounge situated above the Park Row shops. The marble-topped white and gilt bar bears a glittering collection of glasses and a series of great carboy-like cordial flasks. A glazed case contains presentation boxes of Fry's chocolates. The latter were traditionally available in the theatre's saloons. Spittoons on the floor jar with this elegance. Frank Matcham carried out further alterations in 1902. On 24 November 1940 the theatre was destroyed in the Blitz along with the neighbouring Coliseum Cinema.

Monarchs of the Seas

Bristol Museum's superb Prehistoric marine reptiles collection on the first floor of the building (now Brown's brasserie) before its wartime devastation. Although smaller items were moved to safety, the mural fossils proved too unwieldy to rescue. The greatest loss was the holotype of the pliosaurid, Attenborosaurus, renamed in 1993 after the BBC naturalist. A cast of Bristol's original is displayed in London's Natural History Museum. The early and historic collection included fossils found by Mary Anning. In recent years Bristol has again obtained some superb and unique specimens. In the adjoining 1905 Art Gallery, the Bristol Room (now housing Natural History – South West wildlife) appears below arranged for Edward VII's visit in 1908. Edward and Alexandra bravely endured a Corporation lunch below the imposing baldachin on the left. The flowers went to local hospitals afterwards and were replaced by sweet peas for a public showing of the decorations. A total of 20,061 Bristolians viewed it in one day.

Richmond Hill's Museum and Nursery

Naturalist John Charles Stivens opened his Clifton Museum of Natural History 'fronting the Victoria Rooms, with entrance in Richmond Hill' in July 1840. Subscribers enjoyed 6,000 specimens including an 'unsurpassed collection of stuffed English and foreign birds' and 'a beautiful flower garden' overlooking the Rooms. Stivens, of the Italian Warehouse, No. 22 High Street, originally housed his collection at home. Newspapers noted his latest additions from seals and yard-long rats to crocodiles (all shot by himself or acquaintances). In May 1841 he advertised a shipment of Maori and Aboriginal objects for sale. The museum moved to the 'Italian Repository' at No. 1 Fielden Place, Clifton, in 1843. In 1857 all buildings opposite the Rooms were demolished after the land was purchased by subscription. With the proviso that it should never be built on, the land was transferred to the Merchant Venturers. It was a nursery by the 1880s and Forest and Orchard Nurseries when photographed here in 1955.

The Unpleasantness at the Victoria Rooms

An 1830s plan to erect public rooms for gentlemen of all political parties was confounded when Tories threw a 'fit of childish caprice', erecting their own at a cost of £23,000. The foundation stone was laid on the queen's birthday in 1838 and the Victoria Rooms opened on the same day in 1842. The 9-foot Flaxmanesque reliefs of Minerva and Apollo, the Graces and Night and Day encapsulated the projected cultural entertainments. Carriages entered its porte cochère from the Clifton side. Snobbery meant that 1850s Bristol society divided into rival coteries. The Victoria Rooms' group considered itself superior, offensively refusing applications for ball tickets to their 'inferiors'. One 'Patroness' demanded sight of an applicant's marriage certificate before issuing tickets until reminded of her own early days as a laundress. Such ill-feeling ensued that balls were stopped until the 1860s. Newspapers reminded factions that both sides had sprung from trade. By the 1880s a garden occupied the triangular forecourt.

An Era of Change

By the 1850s Whiteladies Road was lined with elegant villas and terraces but, as with most major access routes into cities, these gradually changed from domestic to business use. Guest houses and private schools had always existed in the large properties but now shops started to usurp ground floors. The drawing shows Newbury House, No. 101, an unremarkable terraced house of the 1830s but in 1893, at a time of transition for the road, when private houses jostled with businesses. While still appearing as a house it had been acquired as offices by the estate agents De Ridder and Sons and within a few decades would have a shopfront attached. The drawing shows details of the lost veranda and canopy as well as a pierced stone-fronted terrace before the ground-floor windows. It also appears to have a semi-basement such as survives further south along the street. No. 85 retains a similar fanlight.

'Possessing every accommodation to be found in modern hotels'

The opening of the Clifton Extension Railway to Redland and its subsequent extension to Avonmouth Dock coincided with the development of the Whiteladies Road area. Builder John Thorn formed the North Clifton Hotel Co. Ltd in 1877 to build a new hotel. Messrs Pope and Paul designed the five-storey building on land adjoining Clifton Down Station, acquired from Garaway's nursery. In May 1878 the company issued shares, and the hotel was opened in November, being built in nine months. The principal reception rooms were on the ground floor with the coffee and sitting rooms either side of the main entrance. Maples supplied the hotel's furniture. Of the fifty-eight bedrooms, those on the first floor had *en suite* sitting rooms. Employees and visiting servants had attic rooms while a basement public refreshment room was approached by a side walk. The hotel always had a manageress. The Imperial is now the University of Bristol's Canynge Hall.

'Tyndale Baptist Chapel; to be erected near the turnpike-gate'

The Tyndale Chapel's foundation stone was laid on 17 July 1867. The architect whose 'decorated English style' design had won the architectural competition was Samuel Hancorn of Stephen Street, Bristol and Dock Street, Newport. He died before it opened on 30 September 1868. The opening service was followed by a cold collation at the Royal Hotel. Construction was contracted to Messrs Marquis and Munro of Old Market Street at £5,652 but it eventually cost more. In May 1868 a bazaar and concert at the Victoria Rooms raised funds. The tower was at first only built high enough to enable access to the gallery over the porch. Its completion in 1894 (photographed 1893 and 1905), with Messrs Crisp and Oatley as the overseeing architects, celebrated the Minister's twenty-five years in office. Blitzed in the Second World War, the shell was utilised for a new church designed by Eustace Button in 1957.

A Bristol Society Wedding

Tyndale Baptist Chapel, Whiteladies Road, decorated for the wedding of Ruth ('Ruby') Sargent to Laurence Pascall on 19 July 1911. Ruth was the daughter of the banker Edward Sargent, who had been a Tyndale deacon since 1895. His wife Emily was also closely connected to the chapel for forty-seven years. She was an enthusiastic supporter of the Sunday school and of missionary work, paying for the founding of a missionary station in Africa. These photographs not only show the sort of floral decorations expected at such weddings but are also a useful record of the interior of the chapel that was destroyed in the Blitz. White lilies and daisies predominate. A great bell of white daisies hangs overhead. The upper photograph is taken from the end gallery.

'Almost every article for the use of Gardens'

'Opulence prefers security to taste, and even convenience, for her stone walls inclose the road, and confine the sun-beams and dust to a most pernicious degree' (Malcolm). 'For a considerable way, the road led between stone walls, which bounded the fields on each side. This boundary, tho' of all others the most unpleasing, is yet proper as you approach a great town: it is a kind of connecting thread.' Thus James Malcolm and Charles Heath described Whiteladies Road in the 1800s when most of its length was walled, protecting Miller and Sweet's Nursery (later Garaway's) from the light-fingered. Their Nursery Villas, seen here and originally a 1670s farmhouse, survives in Chantry Road. Miller's 1808 catalogue offered 113 varieties of apples, ninety-nine of gooseberries and fifty-eight different grapevines alone. By the 1970s only their Chantry Road premises and the Severnvale Garden Centre at Richmond Hill survived. Garaway's, opposite the farmhouse, sadly closed in 2008 and was redeveloped.

At the Clarendon, 1914

Apart from the Imperial and the Queen's Hotel, Edwardian Whiteladies Road also boasted several private establishments and boarding houses. The smartest was the Clarendon, opposite St John's church, and near the corner of Burlington road. Run by the Stephens family, it occupied Nos 153–157, the three attached 1856 Italianate villas designed by William Bruce Gingell. The outer houses had bay windows and corner towers while the central one sported a double veranda. The lost front gardens were eclectically bounded by walls topped with a superb Viking scrollwork balustrade and the elaborate gate piers were topped with Scandinavian gables sculpted with curved 'tiles'. Although now offices, the façade of the central house survives remarkably intact. In 1858 the road from Whiteladies Gate was widened and a tree-lined footpath made at the expense of nursery land. Bristol's James Bryan, the founder of Bryan Brothers, was once a waiter here.

'The Church near King's Parade to be called St John's'

Consecrated on 27 April 1841, St John the Evangelist arose on land donated by G. Daubeny Esq. John Hick's 'very neat structure' is in a Tudor-Gothic style, with walls of pink Brandon Hill Grit rubble with limestone dressings and towers. Proving too small for purpose, on June 22 and 23 1859 the Victoria Rooms saw a fundraising bazaar for the building of transepts and a chancel. Their construction in 1864 under S. B. Gabriel raised seating numbers to 1,000, half of which were free. A reredos by J. Buggins of Park Row was added in 1867. Bell and Sons's 1888 north transept window commemorated Revd H. G. Walsh's, forty-seven-year incumbency. Fashionable weddings included that of tragedian William C. Macready in 1860. Closed by 1984, it was subdivided and renamed St John's Court in 1990, with Bristol Auction Rooms on the ground floor and offices above. The 1860s photograph looks towards Whiteladies Road.

St John's Vicarage, 1848

John Hicks' Tudor-style St John's Vicarage (often 'Parsonage') of 1846 at Durdham Down faced the same architect's Church of St John on the corner of Whiteladies Road and Apsley Road. Originally it stood almost alone in fields accompanied by the first two adjoining houses of a later terrace and the few scattered buildings and quarrymens' cottages of Durdham Down hamlet. By 1855, the area was rapidly expanding with roads and villas commemorating by name the Duke of Wellington, who died in 1852. Many properties were designed by Samuel B. Gabriel, who also added to the vicarage. Apsley Row (later Terrace) built next to the vicarage would ultimately name the road itself. A trapezoidal area called Wellington Park behind it may have been planned as just that but by the late 1850s was being developed. Old Vicarage Place and Apsley Mews have now replaced the vicarage and its garden.

Sargents on Parade

Edward and Emily Sargent and their well-connected sons and daughters line the rear veranda of St Austell, No. 80, (later renumbered to No. 94) Pembroke Road in 1899. The house was named after Emily's place of origin. Sargent later had the veranda on the substantial villa extended to the right to front a large bow window and then covered by an iron and glass canopy. He rather reminds one of the retired Pembroke Road banker in Betjeman's amusing poem 'Bristol and Clifton' as he was both a fervent churchman and a financier. However, Emily did not become a victim to the many stairs in supervising servants and in 1912 they happily retired to a rustic life in Ashburnham, one of William Studley's new country villas in Coombe Dingle. St Austell's porch and doors then showed a wealth of stained glass and its façade bore window boxes and was fashionably smothered in ivy and Virginia creeper.

En glad Jul! From Miss Theodora Johnson. Swedish Institute. Clifton

En Glad Jul! From Miss Theodora Johnson

From the 1880s Theodora Johnson, assisted by Frøken ('Miss') Dahl, became synonymous with the introduction of Swedish Drill or physical education to girls and ladies in Bristol and the surrounding areas. She lectured and encouraged and, in 1897, wrote a book on the subject. Johnson established the Swedish Institute for Physical Education at No. 20 Vyvyan Terrace, building 'The Swedish Gymnasium' (decorated with Thorvaldsen reliefs) in its garden in 1893. With Johnson as Principal and such patrons as the Duchess of Beaufort, the Bishop of Bristol and well-known physicians, the institute thrived. It had three departments: Medical, Educational and Dancing. Selected exercise, medico-massage and electricity corrected physical defects. Lectures on physiology and hygiene accompanied developmental physical and mental exercises. Dancing included 'Graceful and Aesthetic movement' and old Swedish peasant dances (shown here). Florence Jenkinson succeeded Nora Gough as Director of Dance. A ballet school from the 1920s, now Bristol School of Dancing occupies the building.